INDIANS OF THE NORTHWEST

TRADITIONS, HISTORY, LEGENDS, AND LIFE

THE NATIVE AMERICANS

INDIANS OF THE NORTHWEST

TRADITIONS, HISTORY, LEGENDS, AND LIFE

PETRA PRESS

COURAGE BOOKS

AN IMPRINT OF RUNNING PRESS
PHILADELPHIA • LONDON

Published in the United States in 1997
by Courage Books, an imprint of
Running Press Book Publishers.

Printed in the United Kingdom by Butler & Tanner Limited

9 8 7 6 5 4 3 2 1

Digit on the right indicates the number of this printing

ISBN 0-7624-0072-2

Library of Congress Cataloging-in-Publication Number 96-69255

THE NATIVE AMERICANS
INDIANS OF THE NORTHWEST
was prepared and produced by
Michael Friedman Publishing Group, Inc.
15 West 26th Street
New York, New York 10010

Editor: Tony Burgess
Art Director: Lynne Yeamans
Layout: Robbi Oppermann Firestone
Photography Editors: Colleen A. Branigan and Deidra Gorgos

Color separations by Ocean Graphic International Company Ltd.

Published by Courage Books,
an imprint of Running Press Book Publishers
125 South Twenty-second Street
Philadelphia, Pennsylvania 19103-4399

10.95

Contents

INTRODUCTION

The First Americans

By the time European explorers arrived in North America in the fifteenth century, many rich, advanced, and diverse cultures had already developed on the continent and had been in existence for a long time. Most historians agree that the first people to inhabit North America arrived more than eleven thousand years ago, having traveled from Asia to Alaska over a land bridge at the Bering Strait. From there, these first Americans eventually traveled and settled throughout North, Central, and South America, where they adapted to the climate and conditions of the land.

In this book we will explore the fascinating cultures of the peoples who lived along the coastline from what is now southern Alaska to northern California, focusing on the life they led before contact with Europeans. Like other first Americans, these Northwest Coast peoples did not leave behind any written records, so archaeologists and historians have had to use other means to reconstruct what their lives were like during the exten-

sive precontact period. Much of this knowledge comes from archaeologists piecing together information based on artifacts, such as tools and ornaments made of stone or bone, that they have discovered. Another important source of information is the oral tradition—stories and legends recounted by Northwest Coast peoples and passed down from generation to generation.

One other way in which historians have been able to understand precontact cultures is by studying the written accounts of early European explorers and missionaries who witnessed the practices and traditions of Northwest Coast peoples before they were influenced by Europeans. These accounts, however, are less reliable than the other two sources mentioned because most Europeans failed to appreciate how rich and highly developed the non-Christian cultures really were. In fact, as we will discover toward the end of this book, it was precisely this outside contact that ultimately led to the decline of Northwest Coast peoples.

THE PACIFIC NORTHWEST

The map below shows the locations of the major
cultural groups that lived on the Northwest Coast.

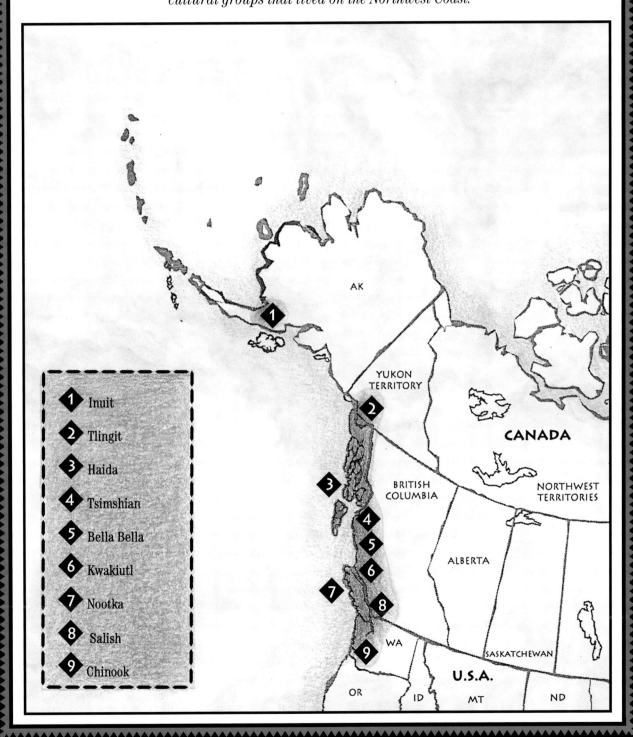

1 Inuit

2 Tlingit

3 Haida

4 Tsimshian

5 Bella Bella

6 Kwakiutl

7 Nootka

8 Salish

9 Chinook

CHAPTER ONE

The Northwest Coast

A Rugged but Hospitable Place to Live

Before learning about the peoples themselves, it is important to understand the climate and terrain of the Northwest Coast, for these elements greatly affected the cultural development of the peoples living there. The Northwest Coast is a narrow strip of coastal land and islands in North America that extends from the mouth of the Columbia River in Washington State up through British Columbia to southeast Alaska. This strip, which is only one hundred miles (160km) across at its widest point, lies between the Pacific Ocean and mountains called the Coast Ranges, which isolate the area from the rest of North America.

At first glance, the region looks like a harsh and hostile place in which to live. In many areas the mountains rise directly from the water's edge and reach snowcapped peaks three thousand to four thousand feet (914–1,219m) high. The only routes across these mountains are passes cut by major rivers such as the Nass, Skeena, and Columbia. Ancient glaciers that long ago pushed their way down the mountain slopes scoured

⚜ OPPOSITE: The mountains towering over British Columbia's Skeena River inspired countless myths and legends among the Tsimshian and Haida peoples. **ABOVE:** Bushes thick with luscious blackberries often grew right along riverbanks, making the berries easy to pick from a canoe. Some berries were eaten fresh, but most were preserved in fish oil for the long winter months.

out a jagged seacoast with hundreds of tiny inlets and fjords, as well as a wide offshore bank of islands that were once the peaks and plateaus of yet more mountains. Some of these islands, such as Vancouver Island and the Queen Charlotte Islands, are extremely large.

Although the geography of the Northwest Coast must not have been very hospitable to early inhabitants, the climate more than made up for the terrain. The summers were relatively cool and the winters were, for the most part, mild and wet. The combination of moderate temperatures and heavy rainfall produced rich inland forests of fir, spruce, and cedar trees. Though the land was not good for farming, there was an abundant supply of game, as well as roots, berries, herbs, and grasses. On top of all these resources was a seemingly endless supply of freshwater fish, saltwater fish, and sea mammals such as seals and whales, which provided more than enough food for even a large population.

Although the climate helped to provide many wonderful resources, it was also the source of some unpleasant surprises. In winter, occasional fierce winds called "williwaws" brought sudden subfreezing temperatures. In summer, the area was often subject to dangerous thunderstorms, whirlpools, crosscurrents, and riptides, all of which made fishing and whaling very dangerous.

Rich and Diverse Cultures

Over the course of several thousands of years following the initial migration across the Bering Strait land bridge, many peoples traveled southward. By 7500 B.C., many had settled on the Queen Charlotte Islands and along the adjacent strip of coastline in the Northwest, where they lived as hunters and gatherers. By 6000 B.C., Northwest Coast peoples were accomplished carvers, using stone tools to make canoes and build massive houses from logs and planking. Bone tools were developed as early as 2000 B.C., and as woodworking techniques improved, Northwest Coast peoples began building large oceangoing canoes, which enabled them to hunt sea mammals. They developed a sophisticated social structure and ceremonial life, and created magnificent artwork.

Because of the narrow beach areas, villages remained, for the most part, small and scattered. Nevertheless, by the fourteenth century the Northwest Coast had between sixty thousand and seventy thousand inhabitants, making it the most densely populated area in North America at that time. There were several main language groups, but because many villages became isolated, a number of tribes within those groups developed their own dialects. While almost all these groups shared certain beliefs and ways of living, each also had its own distinctive myths and ways of dressing, socializing, and waging war.

The Tlingit people were the northernmost group, living along the southern Alaskan coast. They were divided into fourteen tribal groups living in about fifty villages. Their southern neighbors were the Tsimshian cultures, who inhabited villages both along the coast and inland along the major rivers. Because of their strategic locations, the Tsimshian were great traders, dealing in copper and otter skins. Both the Tsimshian and Tlingit cultures were known for their fringed Chiklat blankets woven from shredded cedar bark and the hair of wild mountain goats. These blankets were considered an extremely valuable trade item because of a mystic design woven into them that was believed to give its wearer the power of eloquent and persuasive speech.

OVER THE YEARS, THE MULTIFAMILY WOOD-PLANK LONGHOUSES INCREASED IN SIZE, AND AS WOODWORKING TOOLS BECAME MORE COMPLEX, THE CHARACTERISTIC BOLD AND WAVY ANIMAL DESIGNS CARVED INTO THE POLES AND ENTRYWAYS SUCH AS THIS ONE BECAME EVEN MORE ELABORATE, ESPECIALLY FOR HIGH-RANKING MEMBERS OF THE COMMUNITY.

INUIT AND ALEUTS

Two distinct cultures inhabited some of the northernmost stretches of the Northwest Coast area: the Inuit and the Aleuts. The Inuit (also known as Eskimo) were spread across the arctic and subarctic regions of northern Canada and Alaska. The Aleuts were a separate group that inhabited the string of Aleutian Islands off the southwestern tip of what is today Alaska. Both of these groups possessed languages and cultures totally unrelated to other early North American peoples. Even their physical characteristics were different, resembling the features of northeast Asian peoples. Both Aleut and Inuit cultures had developed amazing ways of adapting to their frigid environment with its long, dark winters and ice cover that never completely melted. They built warm and efficient houses made of ice blocks, constructed skin-covered canoes and watertight kayaks for hunting sea mammals such as seals and sea lions, and developed superior harpooning skills.

A YOUNG INUIT MOTHER WAITS FOR HER HUSBAND'S CANOE ON THE BANKS OF ALASKA'S KUSKEKWIN RIVER WHILE HER BABY SLEEPS, WARM AND SNUG ON HIS CRADLEBOARD.

"COPPERS"—COPPER PLAQUES HAMMERED THIN AND DECORATED WITH PAINTED OR EMBOSSED ANIMAL CRESTS—WERE THE MOST VALUABLE PROPERTY A MAN COULD OWN.

To the south of both the Tsimshian and Tlingit lived the Kwakiutl groups, including such tribes as the Bella Bella and the Heiltsuk. The Kwakiutl originated secret dancing societies that eventually spread to all the other Northwest Coast peoples. They were also excellent wood-carvers.

Off the coast to the west of the Tlingit and Tsimshian groups, on the Queen Charlotte Islands, were the Haida. They were feared by other Northwest Coast groups because of their daring war exploits and their willingness to risk long and dangerous sea voyages to raid other coastal villages for slaves, people whom they would capture and put to work. Like the Kwakiutl, they were famous for their skill in wood carving.

About twenty tribes of the Nootka, another feared and aggressive culture, lived along the coast from the Alaskan Panhandle south to Puget Sound. Aside from their ferocity, the Nootka were famous for their whaling longboats and their superior harpooning skills.

Off the coastal area inhabited by the Nootka were the Salish and Chinook, who lived on Vancouver Island, on islands in Puget Sound, and along part of the coast of Washington State. Some Salish tribes, including the Bella Coola, lived in mainland areas so close to the Kwakiutl that they incorporated both Salish and Kwakiutl elements into their culture. The Salish were known to raid other tribes for slaves that they would then sell to less aggressive groups. Yurok, Karok, and Hupa cultures stretched south from Puget Sound to northern California. These groups occasionally traded with California tribes to the south as well as with other Northwest Coast peoples.

In spite of their language differences and the geography that isolated most villages, trade was an important form of interaction among Northwest Coast cultures. The Chinook tribes, located at the mouth of the Columbia River, acted as middlemen between the peoples of the southern Northwest Coast and other groups. Some tribes traveled by canoe as far as one thousand miles (1,600km) up and down the coast each year (as well as downriver from inland villages) to trade skins, dried salmon, fish oil, copper, canoes, and slaves, as well as beautifully carved and woven items.

What Made Northwest Coast Cultures Outstanding and Unique

The Northwest Coast cultures are considered extraordinary for several reasons. First, they produced a high culture equal to or surpassing that of the Pueblo peoples of the Southwest and the Mound Builders of the Northeast Woodlands—though they had neither agriculture nor pottery, two features usually associated with higher cultures. The tremendous abundance of available food meant that Northwest Coast people never had to learn to farm. Moreover, it gave them much more leisure time than any other early American culture had. By gathering and storing their food supply in summer, they had their entire winter free to hold elaborate dances and ceremonials, throw huge, week-long parties, build houses, carve out canoes, tell stories, wage war, and create wonderful works of art. They developed such highly advanced wood-carving and basket-making techniques that they were able to produce extremely effective cooking implements and containers, and hence had no need for pottery. Gathered around their indoor winter fires, they made utensils, tools, and clothing for everyday use; costumes, masks, and jewelry for winter ceremonials; and the carved crests and clan totems that decorated their houses, canoes, and furniture.

Second, peoples of the Northwest Coast were the only New World cultures uninfluenced by the Aztec and the Maya, the ancient civilizations of Mexico, whose explorers traded with both the Pueblo and Mound Building cultures of North America. Instead of a Mexican cultural influence, many anthropologists believe that the people of the Northwest Coast may have interacted with inhabitants of Northeast Asia. According to those anthropologists, there are many similarities between the mythology and art of the two areas that tend to substantiate the theory.

Third, Northwest Coast peoples were among the few New World cultures to place value on the acquisition of property. Wealth meant social status, and a person's social status, in turn, determined his—and his family's—worth. Unlike most other Native American cultures, the tribes of the Northwest Coast had complex social class systems that divided village populations into various levels of nobility and commoners. Slavery was also common. In some cultures, such as the Nootka, as much as a third of a village population was made up of slaves who had been kidnapped from other tribes up and down the coast.

As we will see in the following chapters, Northwest Coast peoples were exceptionally imaginative and melodramatic. These characteristics are evident in their vividly staged winter ceremonies, their rich mythology, and the exceptional ways in which they adapted to their challenging environment.

CHAPTER TWO

Living Off the Bountiful Land

Northwest Coast peoples needed to be experts at hunting, fishing, and gathering in order to reap the benefits of the land. They also had to build warm winter housing to survive the occasional extremes of weather, and solid canoes to maneuver through river rapids and treacherous ocean currents. But these activities did not go on all the time. When the seasons changed, the ways in which people spent their time changed as well.

Setting Up Summer Homes

Summer was the season during which people of the Northwest Coast caught and collected most of the year's food. They left their villages and traveled in small family groups to fishing spots along rivers and at river mouths. Families rarely spent an entire summer at one river location, but instead traveled to many different parts of a river valley or stretch of ocean coastline, seeking various types of salmon, plant life, and game. Some of the main fishing locations had permanent log frameworks, consisting of poles and crossbeams, to which people attached planks they had brought from home. On the return trip, these planks would be lashed between two large canoes and used to carry the food supply. At other summer fishing locations, people built simple brush shelters for temporary cover or tied poles together and covered them with woven mats. These summer homes were usually just large enough to provide one family with room to sleep and to store the food they were collecting for winter.

Saltwater and Freshwater Fishing

Fishing was so important to Northwest Coast peoples that other tribes that occasionally came into contact with them called them the "Fish-Eaters." They fished for herring, halibut, cod, smelt, trout, perch, and sturgeon, but by far their most important catch was salmon. Every summer, the salmon made their yearly journey from the open sea upstream, sometimes as far as fifteen hundred miles (2,400km), to the river locations where they were born. There the females laid their eggs to produce another generation of salmon. Every village had rows and rows of salmon fillets laid out on tall racks to dry in the sun out of the reach of dogs. Some of the salmon was smoked over the huge fires constantly smoldering along the riverbanks. The drying and smoking processes allowed the salmon to keep through the long winter months.

OPPOSITE: As fishermen prepared freshly caught salmon for winter by drying the fillets on racks or smoking them over smoldering fires, women and children gathered roots, berries, and shellfish. **Left**: Salmon was one of the most important sources of food for Northwest Coast peoples.

THE SALMON NEVER REALLY DIED

Most Northwest Coast peoples believed that salmon were not fish at all but people living in a magic kingdom under the sea. Every summer, the Salmon People sent their young men and women in fish disguise to provide food for the human race.

When a salmon was killed and eaten and its bones were returned to the river where it was caught, the fish immediately returned to its Salmon-Home-Beneath-The-Sea and reverted back to its original form. But if the humans who caught the fish were careless and left the bones where dogs could get them, the fish could not return to its home and the Salmon People would become angry—perhaps angry enough to stop making fish available to humans for food. Therefore people took great care with the bones. Moreover, each tribe had its own ceremony for cooking and cleaning the fish, instructions they had originally received from the Salmon People themselves long ago and passed down from one generation to the next.

It was believed that sometimes a salmon chief would visit a human village in the form of a handsome young man interested in marrying one of the village's young women. So if a handsome young man was missing a finger, toe, or other body part, many people believed it was because he was really a Salmon Person, and the human who caught him when he was a fish did not throw all his bones back into the river after eating him. Hence, someone missing a body part was not shunned by others, as he might have been in other cultures, but was instead treated with great respect.

Adapted from Indian Legends of the Pacific Northwest, *Ella E. Clark (Berkeley: University of California Press, 1953).*

Northwest Coast peoples believed that it was necessary to show respect for the fish that had given their lives so human beings could eat. Before the fishing began in the summer, each village held what was called the First Salmon Rite to thank the Salmon Spirits for providing food. No one ever mistreated or killed fish needlessly, and everyone always returned the bones to the river after the fish were filleted.

Fishermen used a number of different methods to catch river fish, but the most effective means was probably a weir, an elaborate construction of poles and nets that was strung over the width of the river to trap fish. The fish caught in these weirs were then easily speared, clubbed, caught with hooks, or netted from either the shore or catwalks built on top of the weirs. After the fish were caught, the women would clean them. They cut off the heads and tails, which they cooked in boiling water, then dried and toasted the skins over the fire. Part of the flesh was dried for winter use; the rest was dipped in fish oil and eaten raw at the evening meal.

Land and Sea Hunting

In summer, it was not unusual for sea mammals such as seals, otters, porpoises, and sea lions to follow schools of fish inland right into the mouth of a river, which made the mammals easy prey for hunters. Sometimes dead whales were washed ashore by summer storms, providing an unexpected but much appreciated source of food. While there was a lot of game in the dense forests a bit farther inland, there were so many bears, elk, beavers, porcupines, and deer available on the outskirts of their temporary villages that hunters rarely had to venture into the dark, overgrown woods for food. Wolves, cougars, wildcats, and coyotes were also plentiful, but spiritual beliefs prevented most Northwest Coast peoples from hunting these animals.

Traditionally, all-male hunting parties ventured out with special hunting dogs and stalked their prey with bows and arrows. They set ingenious traps for deer and bears, and occasionally they had all the women, children, and dogs from the village form a circle around the hunting area making all the noise they could. This drove the deer out into the open, where they became easy targets for the hunters. Hunters also frequently used traps and nets to catch ducks, geese, seagulls, and other large birds.

Although Northwest Coast fishermen caught saltwater fish such as halibut and cod with lines and hooks, the ocean was far more important for hunting whales and other, smaller sea mammals. This type of hunting was dangerous and required years of training. Eight

THE HUNT BECAME EXCITING AFTER THE ORCA WHALE WAS HIT BY A HARPOON. THE CONTEST COULD GO ON FOR DAYS, THE WOUNDED CREATURE DIVING AS DEEP AS TWELVE HUNDRED FEET (366M) AND THEN BREAKING THROUGH THE WATER'S SURFACE FOR AIR, WHIPPING THE SEA INTO FOAM WITH ITS POWERFUL TAIL AND SPOUTING A TWENTY-FOOT (6M) GEYSER OF BLOOD THROUGH ITS BLOWHOLE, ALL THE WHILE DRAGGING THE CANOE AT A FEROCIOUS SPEED ACROSS THE OCEAN. SOMETIMES, BEFORE IT FINALLY DIED, THE WOUNDED WHALE WOULD TURN AND ATTACK THE BOAT.

THE FINE ART OF HARPOONING

 HARPOONS WERE SOPHISTICATED HUNTING
TOOLS WITH WOODEN SHAFTS THAT DETACHED
FROM THE SHARPENED MUSSEL-SHELL SPEARHEADS
ON IMPACT. A LONG ROPE WAS ATTACHED TO THE
SPEARHEAD, ALLOWING THE INJURED WHALE TO RUN
WITHOUT LETTING HIM GET AWAY.

*The career of a harpooner began when he was
nine or ten years old. Whether his father had
been a harpooner and he wanted to follow in his
father's footsteps, or whether he got the idea on
his own, a boy could not pursue such a career
unless he was chosen during his vision quest (see
page 36) by a special spirit—like the spirit of the
stormy petrel (a seabird that often circles above
whales) or the spirit of the whale itself. If a boy
was chosen, the spirit would teach him songs to
lure whales to his canoe and would show him
the secret herbs to rub on his body to make it*
stronger. *Some people, though, believed a harpooner got his powers through blacker magic,
such as by dancing with skeletons on his back,
stealing human flesh and hiding it in the forest,
or keeping human bones in his canoe.*

*After a boy had been contacted by a whaling
spirit, he began to learn to throw the harpoon,
usually from an adult harpooner. Many years of
training were required. Sometimes an adult harpooner would invite the boy to come along on a
whale hunt and watch. The boy also practiced
going without food and staying awake for long
periods of time, because stalking a whale often
took three or four days.*

*As the boy learned the art of whale harpoon-
ing, he started making (or trading for) all the
equipment he would eventually need. Some of it
might already be in the family if his father or an
uncle was a harpoonist, but he still needed to
have his own. He needed a special thirty- to forty-
foot (9–12m) canoe, as well as different sized harpoons and spears, special ropes, and a number of
sealskin floats to slow down and mark the position of a harpooned whale that was trying to get
away. An expert harpooner had to know exactly
what part of the whale's body to aim for (on top,
just behind the whale's head, or behind a front
flipper). Furthermore, he had to have enough
strength to pierce the skin and several feet of
blubber in order to hit the whale's lung or heart.*

trained men in a single canoe could pursue and kill a fifty-foot (15m) whale using nothing more than mussel-shell harpoons, spruce-root ropes—and a great deal of help from their spirit powers. A whaling crew would usually catch at least two whales each summer, but only the southern tribes along the Northwest Coast actually stalked whales. Although tribes farther north also valued whale meat, bones, and oil, they were content to obtain those items from whales that had been beached in storms or stranded in shallows. The Nootka were particularly famous for both their whaling canoes and their whaling skills.

The whole whale hunt depended on the skill of the chief harpooner, who generally owned the canoe and the equipment, property that took years to make or much wealth to acquire. It was the harpooner who picked the men that would make up the crew, and it was the harpooner who did the actual killing. Not just anyone could be a harpooner; a person had to be chosen by a special spirit as a young boy and had to undergo years of rigorous training. The reward, however, was great. A successful harpooner was held in very high esteem by everyone in his village.

No sea crew could hope to get whales all the time. Three-man canoe teams with smaller and lighter harpoons would hunt lesser game such as otters, seals, sea lions, and porpoises. After spearing these smaller mammals, they would drag

them up to the boat with the harpoon rope and club them to death. Sea lions were the most sought-after sea mammals because their meat was tasty and because their intestines made excellent containers, harpoon floats, and (when dried and twisted) bowstrings. Some sea mammals, such as seals, were prized for their fur, which was used for clothing and trading.

Food Gathering

While men hunted and fished in the summer, women went out in groups to collect other kinds of food. They used baskets and digging sticks to gather berries, roots, grasses, and caterpillars from inland hills and meadows. Roots were dried and then threaded on a string of dried cattail. Thistles were pounded into a sort of flour, which was later mixed with water and baked to make hard loaves that could keep all winter. A piece slathered with fish oil was considered a special treat. Berries such as blackberries and huckleberries were preserved in fish oil, while crabapples were picked green a whole branch at a time, then ripened and dried. Women also used baskets to collect clams, mollusks, and other shellfish along the rocky shorelines. Clams (which were steamed, then

THIS BERRY BASKET WOVEN FROM SPLIT AND POUNDED SPRUCE ROOTS TOOK A TLINGIT WOMAN MANY HOURS SITTING AT A WINTER FIRE TO MAKE.

CANOES MEANT SURVIVAL

Northwest Coast peoples traveled almost exclusively by canoe, both on the ocean and along rivers and streams. Besides using canoes for the general transportation of people and trade goods, they used these vessels for fishing, for hunting small sea mammals, and even for gathering the berries and grasses that grew along riverbanks.

Red cedar was the preferred material for making canoes. In northern areas where only cottonwoods or yellow cedar trees grew, groups like the Tlingit had to import the red cedar or trade with their neighbors to the south for ready-made canoes. Canoes were dug out of single cedar trunks by using stone tools. Canoes came in a great variety of sizes and shapes, depending on their intended use. Some were small, light two-man boats with thin walls and small paddles; others were huge vessels up to seventy feet

(21m) long, strong enough to hold fifty or sixty men in rough ocean currents. Some were even outfitted with sails made out of mats or thin wooden planks. Canoe design varied from north to south, but almost every style featured elegant, carved bows and graceful lines that gave them excellent maneuverability. Sharp-ended canoes were built for rough ocean water and river rapids, while blunt-ended ones were designed for still-water navigation. People took great care of their canoes, oiling the bottoms with seal or fish oil and taking care to beach them where there were no rocks that could damage the hulls.

❧ WHALING WAS A HIGHLY SKILLED PROFESSION THAT DEMANDED COURAGE, STRENGTH, AND PATIENCE. A HEAVY, OCEAN-GOING CANOE AND A STRONG GUARDIAN SPIRIT WERE ALSO VERY HELPFUL.

dried and threaded on strings) were used as articles of trade as well as food, so women spent a lot of time making sure they collected a plentiful supply. Shellfish were either dried or preserved in fish oil for use in the winter.

The Transition to Winter

In late autumn, when the rains began, villagers pulled the roof mats off their summer shelters, or unlashed the wall planks from the summer frameworks, and started packing their stores of food for the canoe ride back home, where they would spend the winter. Families stockpiled such a tremendous amount of dried food and fish oil over the summer that they would not have to leave the house in winter for weeks or even months at a time. As we will see in the next chapters, they spent enjoyable winter days gathered around their blazing indoor fires telling stories, feasting, and creating art. While the women wove baskets and cloth, men carved wood and bone tools, utensils, and boxes. Families, and sometimes whole villages, had time in winter to throw potlatches, elaborate parties where the host gave presents to all his guests (see page 45).

❦ INTRICATELY CARVED SERVING UTENSILS LIKE THIS BIRD-SHAPED KWAKI-UTL LADLE WERE USED ONLY FOR SPECIAL FEASTS.

FISH OIL— MORE PRECIOUS THAN GOLD

Life on the Northwest Coast would have been a lot less pleasant without fish oil. People used it as a sauce, spread, gravy, and salad dressing. It was considered especially tasty with dried or smoked salmon. Furthermore, it was an important source of nutrients. Oil, especially from candlefish, was also valuable as lamp fuel.

People obtained the oil by boiling large quantities of fish in an old canoe filled with water, then skimming the oil as it rose to the surface. After boiling the fish, women would press them against their bodies to squeeze out any remaining oil.

Families stored as much oil as possible each year because the amount of oil a family had was a status symbol that indicated wealth. The more oil a family could afford to burn, the more wealth and status they could claim in the community. Oil was also an important commodity for trade among Northwest Coast tribes, as well as with Plains cultures to the east and California cultures to the south.

Building Winter Homes

Although winters on the Northwest Coast were not snowy, they certainly were wet. Weather conditions varied from a moderately cool, heavy mist to a steady bone-chilling drizzle. People needed solid, warm houses to endure this kind of weather, so that is what they built. Complete with earthen floors and large open spaces that could accommodate several blazing fires at once, their wooden houses were often so huge that they could provide shelter for dozens of families. It took many years and the work of a lot of people to plan and build such a house. Often, a number of families would band together to work on a house and then live in it together. These

🌿 Wooden longhouses were built close to each other on the narrow Pacific coast beaches for protection against warring tribes. The carved totem poles advised strangers if the animal clan members living there were friends or foes.

BUILDING A HOUSE WITHOUT A SAW, NAILS, OR IRON TOOLS

Where it was available, builders preferred to use red cedar, a tough wood that does not decay easily, for their houses. First, the men firmly planted a sturdy framework of posts and cross-beams into the earth. This framework was the permanent part of the house. Then they added wood planks, which were either lashed horizontally to the framework with rope made from stripped cedar bark or simply leaned up against the framework vertically. Either way, the planks were movable so that they could be shifted to make smoke holes. This mobility also made it easy to remove the boards and take them along to the summer fishing camp.

Although the boards could be lashed together tightly, there were always cracks, which were filled with moss until the inside of the house became too smoky. The moss was removed until the house aired out, then stuffed back into the cracks. The entryways to the house were small oval openings several feet off the ground, covered with elk-skin curtains. People had to stoop as they climbed in. These seemingly inconvenient doors were another form of protection against surprise enemy attacks. Although a multifamily house had several doors, it had no windows, so the interior was very dark.

Unless it rotted, a board never lost its value because it could be put up anywhere. The men of a family owned the boards they made for their part of the house, and they took them along when they moved. When they died, they willed the boards to their sons.

🌿 ORIGINALLY, NORTHWEST COAST PEOPLES CHISELED THEIR HAMMERHEADS FROM STONE INTO ANIMAL SHAPES AND LASHED THEM TO LONG WOODEN HANDLES. AMONG THEIR OTHER USES, HAMMERS DROVE WEDGES INTO LOGS TO SPLIT THEM INTO HOUSE BUILDING BOARDS.

large multifamily houses were called "longhouses" by the Salish groups and "bighouses" elsewhere along the coast. In some areas, however, villagers preferred smaller, one-, two-, and three-family houses.

Location was crucial. If at all possible, the groups of houses that formed villages were built on a riverbank, either at the mouth of a river where it flowed into the ocean or at a point upstream where the river flowed into a larger stream. This type of location ensured at least two kinds of fishing (saltwater and freshwater), two water travel routes, and a way to float heavy building logs from the inland forests to village construction sites. A village location also needed to have a safe, smooth place to beach canoes.

Houses were usually built in a row along the shore with larger settlements having two or more parallel rows. One side of a house would face the water and the opposite side would face the forest, thereby providing two good means of escape in case of enemy attack. While a multifamily house was practically a fortress in itself, villagers in some areas preferred the added protection of surrounding their rows of houses with a high post stockade. This sturdy fence not only protected the houses, but also the village's ceremonial halls, work sheds, and sweat lodges.

The planks of ceremonial halls and larger family dwellings were often whitewashed and then painted with magnificent black, red, and blue-green animal symbols to identify the family's clan affiliation. Kwakiutl people painted the entire fronts of their houses, while groups farther north limited the painting to the area around the doorway. In addition to the paintings, houses were often decorated with carved gables, house posts, and entryways. Some groups, such as the Salish, erected separate carved posts (sometimes called "totem poles") next to each house as well as on beachfronts to mark those areas for fishermen out at sea. Like the house paintings, the carvings displayed animal symbols such as the Raven, Wolf, and Bear to indicate the family's clan as well as its social status within the village.

🦪 EVEN AFTER INTERACTION WITH RUSSIAN AND EUROPEAN TRADERS, BELLA COOLA AND OTHER INDIAN GROUPS CONTINUED TO DECORATE THEIR HOUSES WITH TRADITIONAL CLAN SYMBOLS UNTIL THE EARLY 1900s.

Separate work sheds were built next to each house so that men would have a place away from the women to make their tools. Although the need for space was one reason underlying the construction of a shed, another important reason stemmed from the belief that if women saw tools being made, the tools would break during use.

🌿 WINDOWLESS LONGHOUSES WERE DARK AND SMOKY FROM THE INDOOR COOKING FIRES. EACH FAMILY HAD ITS OWN COMPARTMENT ALONG THE WALLS, BUT THE PULL-DOWN STRAW MATS THAT SERVED AS WALLS DID NOT PROVIDE MUCH PRIVACY.

Several pits were dug into the earthen floors for fires, and the huge living space was divided into small family compartments separated from each other by woven straw-mat walls.

The furniture consisted mostly of built-in platforms that could be used as both beds and seats. These platforms wrapped around three sides of each family's compartment and were covered with furs and bird skins. Mats were also used as seat covers, tablecloths, carpets, and blankets. All extra space on the walls and under the platforms served as storage space for the family's belongings and food.

Sweat lodges were also important. These were smaller wooden buildings containing rooms that were closed up tightly and heated with hot rocks to create a saunalike environment. The "bather" would sit in this room until he believed he had sweated all the evil and impurity out of his body. Afterward, he would rub himself with hard twigs and, if it was possible, plunge into a pool of cold water. People routinely took sweat baths for hygienic reasons, but this ritual was also an important part of many tribal ceremonies and spiritual quests.

Northwest Coast peoples used skill and ingenuity to make the most of the area's natural resources and abundant food supply. By working hard each summer to stockpile a large supply of food, they gave themselves plenty of leisure time in winter. This allowed them to enrich their cultures with beautifully crafted artwork, a highly developed spirituality, a close-knit family life, and a unique and complex social system.

CHAPTER THREE

Responsíbílítíes and Daíly Lífe

Even though people of the Northwest Coast lived in communal households of up to forty families, the central family unit, consisting of husbands, wives, children, and grandchildren, was very important. All members of the family, including children and the elderly, had specific tasks and responsibilities. For the most part, men did the building, made canoes, fished, and hunted, while women ran the household and gathered the plants and shellfish that rounded out their diets.

🌿 Taking Care of the Household

Whether living at summer camp or settled in at home for the long, wet winter, one of a woman's primary responsibilities was cooking her family's meals. In summer, food was usually eaten fresh each day after it was caught or gathered. If it was cooked at all, the food was speared with a pointed green stick and broiled on racks over an open fire. In winter, there was plenty of food stored in the family's living compartment, but most of it was dried, smoked, or preserved in oil. This meant that preparing a meal took more time and required special utensils. Occasionally men ventured out in winter to catch dog salmon or collect shellfish, which their wives broiled fresh the same evening. Most of the time, however, preserved winter food had to be baked, steamed, or boiled before being served.

🌿 **OPPOSITE:** DINNER OFTEN MEANT BARBECUING FRESH FISH OVER THE FLAMES OF AN INDOOR FIRE OR COOKING RECONSTITUTED DRIED FISH IN A BOILING BOX SET ON HOT ROCKS.

A TYPICAL MEAL

Northwest Coast peoples had highly developed table manners, washing their hands at least twice before each meal and often several more times during the course of the meal. It was considered vulgar for a person to open his mouth wide enough during dinner to show his teeth.

A typical meal would consist of dried fish that had been soaked overnight in water, then boned, pounded, and boiled until moist and tender. Seaweed or herbs provided a vegetable side dish. Almost all meals were served with a bowl of fish oil, which people used as cream, butter, and salad dressing. Dessert was usually some kind of dried berries, also served with fish oil. Everyone used finger bowls and cedar bark napkins to wash the grease off their fingers between courses. Many coastal people (men and women alike) would smoke after a good meal. Tobacco was not available in that area, but other herbs such as kinnikinnick, salal, and dried alder bark provided flavorful smoke when inhaled through hollow stone pipes.

🌿 SALISH MEN OFTEN CARVED THEIR SOAPSTONE PIPE BOWLS IN THE SHAPES OF BIRDS OR OTHER ANIMAL FIGURES.

Baking was done outside the house because it required a deep pit. First, the women would heat stones in a fire at the bottom of the pit. Then they would lay the food on top of the stones and cover it with leaves and dirt to keep in the moisture. The length of cooking time depended on the toughness of the food. The hard roots of camas plants, which are a type of lily, had to be baked for two or three days, while tender salmonberry shoots took only ten minutes. Sometimes water was added to create a steaming process. The advantage of steaming food was that it retained a lot of flavor.

Boiling was performed indoors on stones heated in a fire. After the fire died down, water was boiled in a special tightly woven basket or wooden boiling box. The dried food cooked in the boiling water until it rehydrated. In addition to baskets and boiling boxes, women needed tongs and ladles for cooking, wooden platters and plates for serving, and spoons for eating—all of which were usually carved by the men.

Women were responsible for serving the food as well. There were generally two meals per day: one at about ten in the morning (after the first five or six hours of work had been completed) and another at sunset. Men ate first, then women and children. If a family was wealthy enough to have slaves, the slaves took over the serving and ate last. If it was a family party, however, everyone would probably eat together.

Women also took care of all the housekeeping, which was especially difficult when family compartments were small and space was limited. Every day, the women would clean the fireplace, fetch water for washing and cooking, and ensure that all utensils, tools, and other possessions were put away properly.

◖ NORTHWEST COAST WOMEN TODAY ARE REVIVING THE CREATIVE AND DEMANDING ART OF WEAVING INTRICATELY DECORATED TRADITIONAL BASKETS.

◖ Basketry, Nets, and Weaving

By the first few centuries A.D., Northwest Coast women had become expert basket makers, weaving baskets that were not only functional but also beautiful, with colored dyes, embroidery, beads, and hundreds of different plaiting designs. Women wove baskets in winter, when they had long hours to sit by the fire and weave, but the preparation actually began six months earlier. The weaving materials—roots, twigs, and grasses—had to be gathered in summer. Roots and twigs had to be soaked, peeled, and split, and grasses had to be cured and dyed. Cedar bark and twigs made the best baskets, but women also used spruce and hazel shoots. Other plants, such as shiny bear grass and grape roots, were used to embroider designs on the finished baskets. Women also employed

basket-weaving techniques to make the all-purpose cattail mats, as well as the string, heavily braided cords, and nets the men used for hunting and fishing each summer.

Another artistic specialty of Northwest Coast women that had developed by the first few centuries A.D. was weaving cloth. They were the only Native Americans north of Mexico to use wool, which they sheared from the coats of mountain goats and dogs to spin a two-ply yarn. This yarn was then woven on intricate looms into colorful cloth. The cloth, in turn, was used to make clothing and ceremonial blankets. The woven cloth was decorated with embroidery, beads, and many different weaving designs.

RAISING WOOL DOGS

Mountain goat wool was ideal for making yarn, but wild goats could not be found in all areas of the Northwest Coast. Sometimes women obtained goat wool through trade, but more often they raised a special breed of dogs called wool dogs. Kept separate from the house and from hunting dogs, wool dogs were raised solely for their thick fleece. Wool dogs were small and usually white or brownish black. They belonged only to the women, who kept them penned up like sheep and took them along when it was time to move to the summer camps.

LEFT: EVEN THE WEAVING TOOLS WOMEN USED WERE CARVED WITH DECORATIVE ANIMAL DESIGNS LIKE THIS SALISH SPINDLE WHORL, USED TO PREVENT WOOL FROM SLIPPING OFF THE SPINDLE. **BELOW**: BELLA COOLA WOMEN WOVE CEREMONIAL APRONS FROM POUNDED CEDAR BARK STRIPS, THEN DECORATED THEM WITH EMBROIDERY, BEADS, AND EVEN PAINTED WOODEN MASKS.

Women in some tribes also wove blankets and capes from cedar bark that had been stripped from young saplings, soaked for ten days in salt water, and then beaten until flat. The fibers were tightly woven on a special loom to create a soft fabric. Sea otter fur or goat wool was often added as a decorative border.

Carving

In addition to hunting and fishing, men were responsible for all the woodwork, from building houses and canoes to carving finely decorated tools, pipes, ceremonial masks, chests, and cooking utensils. They carved canoes out of fifty-foot (15m) cedar trunks on the beach in the summer, saving most of the smaller projects for winter, when they spent long hours sitting around the indoor family fire or carving tools in their work sheds.

Northwest Coast peoples used various tools for carving. A chisel was fashioned by lashing an animal's horn to a shaft of wood with cedar bark twine. A hammer was made out of a hard stone called dolerite. Northwest Coast peoples also used an adze, which consisted of a D-shaped handle and a horn or stone blade.

Although the Northwest Coast peoples never developed pottery, their baskets and carved

WOODWORKING

Northwest Coast craftsmen could make the most amazing boxes and chests out of wood—without using either nails or a saw. They developed two totally unique methods: bending wood and sewing it.

To bend a wood plank for a square box or chest, craftsmen steamed the wood until it was pliable and then used hot rocks to bend four corners into it. To join the two sides in the fourth corner, they bored holes in the edges of both sides and used cedar rope to sew or lace them together. Sometimes wood pegs were used instead of the lacing cord. After the four sides of the box were finished, grooves were chiseled into a bottom piece so that it could be snugly fitted into the box without sewing. Lids were made in the same way. These boxes were so well constructed that water could be boiled in them without leaking.

wooden bowls served all the same purposes quite well. Bowls were usually carved in a canoe shape. Everyday dinner bowls were about a foot (30cm) long, while special feast dishes were three to four feet (91 to 122cm) in length. Many of these dishes were decorated with carved figures and inlaid with shells or teeth. Men also carved spoons, buckets, boiling boxes, and the small bowls used to serve fish oil. Some were carved from wood and polished with sharkskin; others were carved from whale bones  or goat horns. These items became valued possessions.

⚘ Coppers

Men were also responsible for creating "coppers," elegantly decorated and skillfully fashioned thin copper slabs that were distributed with great ceremony at feasts called "potlatches." Because copper could not be found in the Northwest Coast, the peoples there acquired this metal through trade with the Native cultures living farther east. Once men had obtained the copper, they would hammer it into a thin V-shaped form. Then they would hammer various bulges and ridges into the slab. Often Northwest Coast men also engraved or painted traditional animal motifs on coppers.

Games and Sports

Northwest Coast peoples loved athletic games, as well as games of chance on which they could bet. One popular athletic game was called Hoop and Pole, in which competitors tried to shoot pointed sticks through a ring rolling along the ground. Wrestling was also popular, along with arm and finger wrestling. People also loved ball games, especially Shinny, a game like field hockey with hooked striking sticks and wooden balls. Many of these games had no rules against striking other players to make points, and as a result they were often quite rough. Ball games were so popular that some cultures, such as the Coos, had traveling ball teams that played the teams of other villages in front of crowds of cheering fans.

Clothing

Summers were so mild along the Northwest Coast that most women wore only short fringed skirts made of cedar bark. These skirts were lightweight and cool, and dried quickly if the woman was caught out in the rain. Men wore either nothing at all or, if they were fishing in the rain, a protective cape woven from cattails or cedar bark. Both men and women generally went barefoot in the summer, wearing leather moccasins only for special occasions.

GAMES OF CHANCE

By far the most popular game of chance was one in which a player had to guess which of two bags of sticks contained the one called the "ace."

The game started with one player dividing up the sticks from one of his sets into two bundles, which he then wrapped in cedar bark. The other player was supposed to determine from the expression on his opponent's face which bundle contained the single unpainted stick. If he guessed right, he won the set and it was then his turn to set out bundles of sticks.

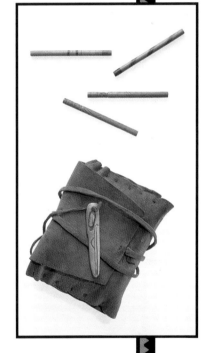

These games often went back and forth with nobody winning for days on end, and the players would barely stop to eat or sleep. Other popular games of chance were played with balls and dice.

ABOVE: HAIDA GAMBLERS OFTEN CARRIED THEIR GAME STICKS IN BEAUTIFULLY FASHIONED LEATHER AND BONE POUCHES.

During the winters, people protected themselves from the elements with everyday clothing made from watertight buckskin. For special occasions, such as ceremonies and potlatches, they wore cream-colored capes woven from goat or dog wool, or Chilkat blankets made from wild mountain goat fur and decorated with duck or loon feathers. Ceremonial fashion varied from group to group. Men in some tribes preferred to wear belted robes, called dance aprons or waist robes, made from buckskin or otter fur. Others wore cattail capes and fringed leggings. Only the wealthy wore beautifully designed woven and sleeved coats.

Shoes were not particularly important, but headgear was. Hats were usually made of woven basketry or carved wood. The wide cone-shaped design was both functional and fashionable. While the large brim protected the person from rain, the number of rings on the top of the hat indicated how many potlatches a man had given, an emblem of both his wealth and his social status. Whether made of basketry or wood, the hats were usually colorfully painted with animal designs. They were important for both social and ceremonial occasions and were even worn by children.

⚜ Body Decoration

It was customary on the Northwest Coast for both men and women to decorate their bodies (and sometimes their faces) with paint and tattoos. Each culture had its own preferred colors and designs. The paint was made by mixing ground-up roots and berries of different colors with bear grease. When preparing for a party or ceremony, people often spent two or three hours applying facial paint.

Jewelry was another important form of adornment. Necklaces, earrings, and other ornaments were made out of beaver teeth, clam and abalone shells, and bear claws. Both men and women had pierced ears, and often pierced noses and lower lips. One of the most unusual ornaments worn by Northwest Coast peoples was the labret, or lip plug, a round or oval disk made of carved stone or bone that was inserted into a hole in a person's lower lip to make his or her lip protrude. These labrets were considered very attractive and were usually reserved for the wealthy. What's more, the size of the lip plug reflected its owner's social status in the community.

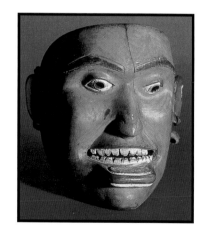

⚜ **Above**: Each culture had its own distinctive ceremonial dress. This affluent Nootka tribesman is wearing a tightly woven basketry hat painted with whale-hunting motifs. **Right**: Several thousand years b.c., wealthy men and women along the Northwest coast began wearing labrets—plugs of stone or inlaid wood buttoned into a hole pierced and stretched in the lower lip. The older and more respected the person, the bigger the labret. By the seventeenth century, only wealthy women among the Tsimshian wore labrets. **Opposite**: Many Tlingit groups continued their winter dances long after the arrival of white traders. This five-year-old Tlingit boy's ceremonial dance dress includes a nose ring.

CHAPTER FOUR
Growing Up

In Northwest Coast cultures, different stages of life, such as childhood, adolescence, adulthood, and old age, were accompanied by specific practices and rituals. Education, rites of passage, marriage, and the burial of the dead were all fundamental aspects of Northwest Coast life, just as they play important roles in societies of today. The ways in which Northwest Coast peoples raised their children and dealt with important turning points, such as the transition from childhood to adulthood, reflected both practical needs and spiritual beliefs.

Newborns

Parents in the Northwest Coast took great care in nurturing their babies. They bathed them daily, rubbed them with whale oil, powdered them with willow ash powder, and wrapped them in disposable cedar bark diapers. Many villages had special baby doctors, who had learned through spirit visions how to diagnose and treat infant diseases. A baby spent the first year of its life strapped to a cradleboard made out of a hollowed-out cedar board filled with soft, shredded cedar bark. The cradleboard enabled a mother to keep her child with her at all times, either carrying it strapped to her back or leaning it against a tree trunk while she was out gathering roots and berries. The board was more than just portable, safe, and comfortable; it was also an effective forehead flattener. A broad forehead and cone-shaped head were considered a mark of both high class and beauty, and a baby's head could easily be molded into that shape by laying a board over the baby's fore-

OPPOSITE: FATHERS TOOK GREAT PRIDE IN GIVING AWAY COPPERS, BLANKETS, AND OTHER VALUABLE GOODS IN HONOR OF THEIR SONS AT SPECIAL POTLATCHES.

BABYLAND

Many Northwest Coast people thought that baby souls came from a land of their own, where they lived and played without any adults. This land was called "Babyland." The people believed that when an infant started its life on earth, it was still speaking the language of Babyland—a language only other babies could understand—but then later forgot it upon growing.

If the baby liked life on earth, he or she would grow up to be a normal adult. But if for some reason he did not, he would choose to die and his soul would return to Babyland to play with other souls until he felt like returning to earth again. Parents believed, therefore, that if they did not keep their babies happy and take the time to learn what they liked and disliked, the babies would die. Parents were also careful to keep an infant who became ill away from other small children because the baby might convince his small friends that they would all be happier back in Babyland.

head and attaching both sides of it securely to the cradleboard. This was done for only the first few months of the baby's life and did not cause the baby any pain. A baby was kept on a cradleboard until it was ready to walk.

The Early Years

During their first five years, children were left in the care of grandparents much of the time. They were given much affection and very few rules or restrictions. When a child reached the age of six, he or she was old enough to follow the father or mother around to start learning grown-up tasks and responsibilities. Boys began to learn the basics of fishing, whaling, hunting, and wood-carving, while girls started learning housekeeping skills and the arts of basketry and weaving. About this time they also started their spiritual training, which included daily ritual baths in cold water, and learning their tribe's legends and creation stories. Children were taught to be quiet indoors and to respect their elders.

Children were never scolded for making mistakes as they learned, but they were always praised when they learned to do something correctly. Parents rarely used physical punishment when their children misbehaved; they found psychological methods much more effective. One common method was telling scary stories of the bogeymen who ate naughty children.

The Vision Quest

In many Northwest Coast cultures, when a boy was considered old enough and knowledgeable enough by tribal elders, he would make a vision quest for a guardian spirit. (In some cultures, girls as well as boys

ABOVE: ONE WAY TO KEEP YOUNGER CHILDREN FROM WANDERING TOO FAR FROM HOME WAS TO TELL THEM BOGEYMAN STORIES. THIS MASK REPRESENTS TSONGA, AN UGLY, WHISTLING GIANTESS WHO SUPPOSEDLY KIDNAPPED STRAY CHILDREN AND ATE THEM.
RIGHT: THE WOLF WAS ONE OF THE MOST POWERFUL AND RESPECTED GUARDIAN SPIRITS A YOUNG BOY COULD RECEIVE ON HIS VISION QUEST.

embarked upon this quest.) This spiritual journey usually occurred during a young person's early teens. The youth would blacken his skin with charcoal and wander alone to a secluded spot far from the tribe. For five or more days, he would fast, brave the elements, and pray to the Great Spirit. During this period of danger and fasting, the first animal, bird, or reptile that he dreamed of when he fell asleep or that came to him in a waking vision was the one the Great Spirit had designated to be his special protector for life. An Eagle spirit, for example, brought the power to become a chief, a Grizzly Bear made a man a warrior, and a Hawk provided luck in gambling. It was believed that a boy who experienced such a vision and found his guardian spirit acquired tremendous power and would achieve many things in his life. But not all the young people who went out on these quests received a spirit vision. Some tried for years before they succeeded; some never experienced one at all. Those who were not contacted by a spirit were much less likely to be successful warriors, medicine men, or hunters.

Marriage

Girls on the Northwest Coast were considered ready for marriage at the age of fourteen, while boys were eligible at sixteen. In the years before her marriage, a girl was expected to be modest and industrious in order to prove what a good wife she would be. The only contact a girl had with boys her own age occurred at ceremonies in the communal hall. Although they were not allowed to talk to each other, many boys and girls became attracted to one another by eye contact alone. Later, when everyone else was asleep, a boy might express interest in a girl he had met by handing a gift to her through an opening in the wall near her

DIVORCE

Divorce was easy, but not common. If a woman discovered that her husband had been unfaithful, she could divorce him by simply leaving and taking the younger children with her. If the wife had been unfaithful or left her husband without good cause, the husband could divorce her, but he was also within his rights to cut off the tips of her nose and ears—or use any other means of discipline he saw fit. When a couple divorced, regardless of how long ago the wedding had been, all their wedding gifts had to be returned.

bed. If she liked the boy enough to accept the present, the boy would propose marriage. But he would make his proposal to the girl's family, not to the girl herself, and the marriage negotiations would begin. The girl's family had to prove that she was the boy's social equal, and they had to offer a sufficient dowry. If the boy agreed to all this, the parents of the bride-to-be made the wedding plans.

The wedding consisted of a three- to four-day feast filled with speeches, rituals, and a great deal of celebrating. A daughter's wedding was a father's chance to throw one of the biggest parties of his lifetime. After several days of gift-giving and rejoicing, the bride was escorted to the beach by male guests who sang while carrying her wedding gifts down to the water, where they were loaded into the groom's canoe.

Having more than one wife was an accepted tradition for men who could afford to do so. Even wealthy men, though, rarely had more than four or five. The only stipulation was that the new wives had to be sisters of the first wife or at least come from the same household.

❧ Old Age and Death

As people grew older, they did less and less heavy work, but they were far from being considered useless. They became the teachers who trained children in both career and spiritual matters and the storytellers who handed down the tribe's legends and creation myths to younger generations. As tribal elders, they presided over important ceremonies, gave counsel, and enjoyed caring for the younger children while the mothers were out gathering food.

Instead of keeping all their property until they died and then bequeathing it to their sons and other relatives, older people began giving away their possessions as soon as they stopped working. A man generally gave his canoe and hunting dogs to one of his sons. He either divided his slaves and other forms of wealth among the rest of his relatives or gave them away at potlatches. Only his personal property remained, and that was buried with him when he died.

Burial customs varied up and down the Northwest Coast, but almost all the cultures maintained cemeteries. The dead were not buried, for it was difficult to dig graves in the forests and sandpits. Instead, they were raised above the ground, usually on the tops of trees. The Nootka and southern Kwakiutl placed the bodies of their dead in large boxes and then put the boxes high up in trees. The Salish also "buried" their dead in treetops, but used canoes instead of boxes. The Tsimshian people cremated their dead—except for the deceased person's heart, which they removed and buried in the ground.

PROTECTION AGAINST THE DEAD

People of the Northwest Coast did not believe in heaven and hell. Instead they believed that the dead went to a comfortable place where they had enjoyable activities and good food to eat.

But they also thought that many of these dead souls were lonely, missing their families and friends so much that they would return to take one of the living back to the land of the dead for company. Since the danger was greatest for the relatives closest to the deceased, the family

hired "undertakers" who bathed and wrapped the dead person, gave him an elaborate funeral, and then buried him according to appropriate tribal custom—without the family having to be present.

If a person died indoors, it was important to remove wall planks and take his body out of the house through the resulting gaps. If the deceased was carried out through the door, he might remember the way and come back looking for his loved ones.

Whatever the burial method, almost all Northwest Coast tribes erected carved wooden monuments (or mortuary columns) near the burial places of their most important citizens.

It was the custom to remove a deceased person's name from the language because saying the words out loud would call back his spirit from the dead. For example, if the man was named Great Bear, people in his tribe could no longer use the word *bear* to describe the animal, but had to use other words instead. If another person had the same word in his own name, he had to adopt a new name.

🌿 **ABOVE**: IN THIS ANCIENT HAIDA CEMETERY, THE CARVED MORTUARY POLES OF EIGHTEENTH-CENTURY TRIBESMEN TOWER OVER THE MORE MODERN MARBLE GRAVESTONES NOW USED BY MANY NORTHWEST COAST NATIVES. **LEFT**: THE BODIES OF TLINGIT CHIEFS WERE OFTEN PLACED INSIDE COFFINS CARVED TO RESEMBLE KILLER WHALES AND SET ATOP CARVED WOODEN MORTUARY POLES.

CHAPTER FIVE

Living in Society

Almost every Northwest Coast culture had a social structure that was divided into various classes of commoners, nobles, and slaves. Social status, which was of the utmost importance, did not apply to individuals but rather to families and clans. While titles of nobility were highly regarded, they were based entirely on wealth. If a family lost its possessions, any titles of nobility that its members might have held would no longer carry any weight in the community. But the reverse was also true: a poor family could improve its social status and even attain the ranks of nobility upon suddenly striking it rich. Only slaves had no potential for advancement.

Families and Clans

The basic social element of all Northwest Coast cultures was the household. Usually made up of dozens of individual families occupying a single communal building, a household functioned as a self-contained social and economic unit. Everyone living in the house was related by either blood or marriage. In many cultures, members of a household were also related by clan. A clan was a group of people who claimed to be descendants of the same legendary spirit ancestor. The Tlingit people, for example, had two major clans: the Ravens and the Wolves. The Tsimshian, on the other hand, were divided into Raven, Eagle, Wolf, and Bear clans. Every clan had its own history, traditions, myths, and legends, as well as a clan crest. Each major clan was divided into about thirty subclans, with such names as Eagle-Frog and Dog-Fish that were based on the other animal spirits playing an important part in the subclan's history. Households that belonged to the same clan often joined forces in times of war or celebration, and a member of a clan knew he could count on support and protection from other members even if they were complete strangers who belonged to a different tribe or spoke a different language.

Marriage within and between these family and clan groups could be complicated. Most of the northern cultures were matrilineal, while those in the south were patrilineal. Some cultures in the middle, such as the Kwakiutl, used both systems. In a matrilineal culture, the husband went to live with the bride's family. The children of the couple were considered to be members of the mother's family and tribe, not the father's. In a patrilineal culture, the opposite was true: the wife went to live with her husband's relatives, and their children became members of the father's family and clan, not the mother's. In some cultures, people were forced to marry someone in a clan other than their own to make sure that every household had members of more than one clan.

OPPOSITE: THE "SPEAKER" OF A HAIDA VILLAGE WAS USUALLY THE ONE IN CHARGE OF DISTRIBUTING BLANKETS AND OTHER GIFTS AT A CHIEF'S POTLATCH. **ABOVE:** THE CARVED WOODEN MASK OF THE KWAKIUTL RAVEN CLAN

CLAN CRESTS AND TOTEM POLES

Representations of legendary beings, such as the Raven and the Wolf, were called "totems." These were carved into clan crests, used to decorate everything from houses to chests to canoes.

Probably the most widespread of these crest carvings was the totem pole. Intricately carved, these towering poles served a number of different functions on the Northwest Coast. They were erected as memorials to show the history of the family's lineage and to commemorate special events. Sometimes they were used as graves for important people: a chief's coffin could be secured in a fork at the top, or the ashes of a wealthy nobleman could be stashed in a secret opening.

Totem poles were also used as household entrances, with a large hole carved in the base for people to walk through. Some of these entrances were carved to represent ravens' beaks that actually opened for people to pass through and then closed again with the help of a complicated set of ropes and pulleys.

The topmost figure on the totem pole always represented the major clan affiliation. Below, other animal figures that played important parts in the clan's mythology would be carved. If more than one clan lived in a communal household, the clan totem of the household's leader was carved at the top, followed by the totems of the others in order of their social status. These totems let people know who lived in a particular house. If a stranger came across members of his own clan, he could always be assured of receiving food, protection, and shelter from them.

🌿 **LEFT AND ABOVE**: BEAUTIFULLY CARVED AND PAINTED TLINGIT TOTEM POLES WERE OFTEN BUILT RIGHT INTO THE FRAME OF A HOUSE AND SERVED AS AN IMPRESSIVE HOUSEHOLD ENTRANCE.

Social Classes

At the top of the social ladder was the family of the tribal leader. However, the status of chief was not achieved by leadership qualities. Instead, the village's leader acquired his position by being the wealthiest man in the community.

Directly under the chief's family were the families of the so-called nobles, the other extremely wealthy families. The Quinault called these people "close-together-chief," while the Coos referred to them as "good people." Usually the families in this class rose to power through their business efforts. If a man's family collected enough dried fish and roots every summer in order to have a large surplus that could be traded for blankets, canoes, slaves, and other important possessions, his family could eventually gain enough wealth to join the higher social circles. Certain skills, such as woodworking, harpooning, and elk hunting, were so valuable that professionals could obtain wealth by teaching these talents to some-

A CAREER IN GAMBLING

It was common for a family to become wealthy through gambling. On the Northwest Coast, people did not gamble on card and dice games just to have fun. For many, it was their lifelong profession. Often men were given the spirit power for gambling on their vision quest.

Professional gamblers played either individually or on teams, often representing their home village against a neighboring one. They were constantly traveling up and down the coast in search of the highest stakes. But they were not the only ones betting on themselves and their gambling skills; their neighbors bet on them as well. A gambler, professional or amateur, could win a fortune for his family or just as easily be financially ruined.

🍃 TOTEM CARVERS WERE HIGHLY SKILLED ARTISTS WHO USED STYLIZED ANIMAL DESIGNS UNIQUE TO THEIR OWN PARTICULAR CULTURES.

one who could afford to pay for lessons. Some elite professions, however, were so treasured and guarded that many cultures would not let poor people or slaves be educated in them. In wealthy families, men holding skilled professions would encourage their sons to learn the same skills or, if a boy was given a spirit guardian with a different calling, at least set them up in business. Families of women skilled at weaving blankets and baskets also had an economic advantage because these articles were valuable commodities that could be traded.

In many Northwest Coast cultures, families were continually making and losing fortunes and, hence, moving from one social class to another. In other cultures, however, tribal rules made it difficult for the lower classes to break out of poverty. In some tribes, village woodworkers would even refuse to help poorer families build houses, forcing them to live in small huts at one end of town, usually at the point where an enemy would most likely strike first. Yet even these cultures had success stories of poor families who rose to the top.

Tlingit baskets like this one, woven out of shredded spruce roots, were decorated with embroidered animal designs.

Slavery

At the bottom of the social ladder were the slaves. The abundant food supply and comfortable climate that provided Northwest Coast peoples with surplus trade goods also gave them enough wealth to buy and feed slaves. Some of the wealthier families kept slaves as personal servants. Others used them as workers in their businesses or to help them hunt. But the true value of slaves was in the fact that they were symbols of wealth. (They often ate more food than they gathered.) The more slaves a family owned, the wealthier the family seemed.

Some slaves were captives of war, but most were members of other tribes who had been seized by raiding parties formed for the purpose of acquiring slaves. The Chinook raided the Oregon coast for slaves, while the Klallam, Lummi, and Cowlitz attacked the peaceful inhabitants of Puget Sound. The feared Tlingit and Nootka tribes pirated slaves up and down the coast from Canada to California. Sometimes two neighboring tribes, such as the Makah and Quilleute, would continually raid each other for slaves. Even the most peaceful tribes, who would never raid other villages, had no qualms about buying slaves from the ones who did.

Bands of slave raiders would sneak up on small encampments at night. There they would try to kill off all the men, old people, and babies, and make off with the young women, girls, and ten- to twelve-year-old boys who were old enough to work but too young to put up much of a fight. Sometimes raiders would sneak up on women who were out alone gathering roots or clams. If the kidnappers were particularly daring—or just plain lucky—they would snatch the daughter of a tribal chief. The ransom he would pay for the return of his daughter was often much greater than the price she could have been sold for as a slave. For the most part, though, no one bothered to rescue or ransom captured slaves at all. Tracing relatives who had been kidnapped was a difficult, if not impossible, task, especially if they had been bought and sold a number of times after having been captured. Even if a slave managed to escape, his family would not welcome him back, because once a person had been a slave, he was considered disgraced for life.

Sometimes people were sold into slavery by their own families. Poor families often resorted to selling their children, nieces, and nephews. If a gambler were desperate enough, he could use himself and/or his family as the stakes for a bet. If he lost, he and/or his family would become the winner's slaves. Unlike others, however, a gambler was usually allowed to work so he could buy himself and his family back out of slavery.

Some tribes, such as the Nootka, often killed slaves as a barbaric show of wealth and power. In most cultures, however, slaves were not so harshly treated. While they were forced to carry out the hardest physical labor, they worked side by side with their masters and were not generally whipped, starved, or punished, mainly because these actions would diminish a slave's ability to work. Slaves generally lived in the same houses as the families they served, ate the same food, and wore the same kind of clothes.

🌿 Potlatches and the Feast System

The potlatch was a feast given to celebrate any sort of occasion such as marriage, the naming of children, coming of age, and announcements of people acquiring titles of nobility. The host of a potlatch distributed extravagant gifts to his guests to demonstrate his own wealth and prestige. By giving away valuable property, he proved that he was worthy of

his particular social position. While ordinary men with moderate amounts of wealth gave smaller potlatches, chiefs gave huge ones, inviting both friends and enemies from villages so distant that the guests had to travel days by canoe.

Families often worked and saved for years in order to throw a potlatch, making baskets, weaving blankets, collecting skins, and carving masks, utensils, and other costly possessions to give away. Because a family's status was based on wealth, it was not uncommon for people to give potlatches they could not afford, just so people would think they had more money than they really did.

The word potlatch comes from the Chinook word *patshatl*, meaning "to give away." Items traditionally given away included everything from blankets, baskets, and furs to carved chests, plates, spoons, weapons, and even slaves. Filled with feasting, singing, dancing, and games, potlatches could last five or more days. On the last day, the gifts were given out by the village speaker on behalf of the host. The kind of gift a guest received was determined by his status; the wealthier the guest, the more extravagant the gift. Enemies received especially luxurious presents.

🌿 HAIDA HELMETS TRADITIONALLY HAD A WOODEN, COPPER, OR WOVEN CYLINDER ON THE TOP DECORATED WITH RINGS TO INDICATE THE NUMBER OF POTLATCHES ITS WEARER HAD ALREADY THROWN. THIS HELMET WITH ITS PROTRUDING BACK "FIN" IS DESIGNED TO REPRESENT A KILLER WHALE.

This custom of gift-giving was not as strange as it might seem. First of all, a lavish party impressed everyone with the host's wealth. Second, every present given to a guest would be paid back some day with a present that was just a little bit nicer. And third, the host proved he was superior to his enemy because he was wealthy enough to give him such an expensive gift. The enemy would then in turn have to invite him to an even more extravagant potlatch and give him an even more expensive gift. It was possible to bankrupt one's enemies this way, thereby achieving a great victory.

Although potlatches could be occasions of great celebration and rejoicing, they were not always thrown for the enjoyment of guests. Instead, some were deliberately hostile and even violent. At such events, rival clan leaders would sing insulting songs to each other and destroy their own valuable property in front of their enemies just to prove they had so much wealth they could afford to throw it away. This often included burning large amounts of precious fish oil, breaking highly prized ceremonial copper plates, and in some cultures, such as the Nootka, even sacrificing slaves. Those who were defeated in these contests of wealth would return to their villages in deep humiliation.

Trade and Money

People traded up and down the entire Northwest Coast, but most of the trade took place in the larger seacoast villages. Inland people paddled downriver to the coastal trading centers with sheepskins, sheep horns, and buckskins. People traded dried foods (such as salmon or shellfish), carved dishes, sea otter pelts, beautiful canoes, fish oil, slaves, baskets, blankets, and other items.

Strings of beads made from dentalia were sometimes used as a sort of shell money. Dentalia are extremely rare, tiny white shells found in deep water off the coast of Vancouver Island. When the beads were not being used for trade, they were worn as earrings and necklaces and used for gambling stakes.

Government

The leader of a village had to be rich because it was his responsibility to take care of the poor and old people without families and to pay all the expenses for village celebrations. In addition to being wealthy, the village leader needed to be a kind and fair man because he was expected to settle local disputes between households and to avoid wars with neighboring villages. Villagers did not pay taxes, but wealthier families generally contributed a part of their hunting bounty to the village leader.

In addition to a leader, each village had a speaker. A man holding this position needed to have a loud voice and the ability to speak several dialects. It was the speaker's responsibility to deliver speeches, hand out gifts at potlatches, and meet with the leaders of other villages.

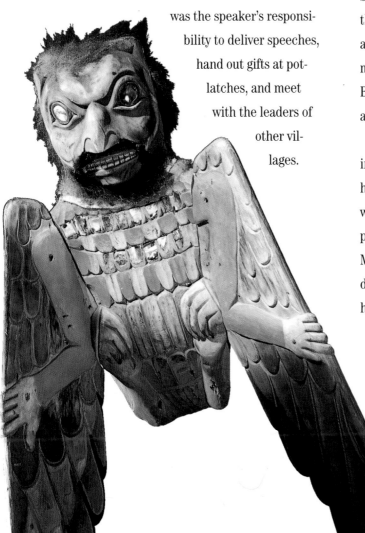

Although villages did not have actual laws, they often had very effective systems of fines for all offenses ranging from insults to murder. Some people attempted to achieve justice through physical violence and witchcraft.

War and Peace

Some groups, such as the Nootka, were more warlike than others. They wore slat armor with wooden helmets as well as carved masks designed to terrify their enemies, and they fought with arrows, spears, and clubs. Before conducting a raid, they sang magical war songs around a campfire.

Northwest Coast peoples had a unique way of making peace. When a war was over, both winners and losers had to pay for the damages. Each side counted up dead warriors and damaged property. Then each side had to pay the other an appropriate amount of compensation. Men who died wealthy were worth more than those who died poor. The payments were divided among those who had fought.

🌿 LEFT: THIS CARVING OF OWL-MAN, A LEGENDARY SPIRIT, WAS A PROW ORNAMENT ON A TLINGIT WAR CANOE. THE FINELY CARVED WOOD IS DECORATED WITH ABALONE SHELLS AND BEAR FUR. ABOVE: TLINGIT WARRIOR HELMETS, LIKE THIS ONE REPRESENTING A RODENT, WERE USUALLY CARVED OUT OF WOOD AND THEN DECORATED WITH PAINT AND HUMAN HAIR.

CHAPTER SIX

Mythology and Spiritual Beliefs

Belief in Supernatural Beings

Native Americans of the Northwest Coast shared their world with spirits. These spirits took many different forms, including pebbles, rocks, trees, animals, the sun, the moon, lakes, rivers, lightning, wind, and rain. Everything possessed a power or spiritual force that human beings could communicate with in dreams and trances. Many of these forces were good spirits who had the power to help and protect people. Others, however, were evil, plotting to kill those who were lost or unprotected.

The evil spirits generally lived in wild places deep in the forests, under the seas, or on mountaintops. In the mountains, there was *Baxbakualanuxiswae* (the Cannibal-at-the-North-End-of-the-World), whose household included an evil seductress who lured men to their doom; a man-eating bird with an immense, bone-breaking beak; and a huge, supernatural grizzly bear. The sea was home to horrible two-headed serpents, man-eating giant squid, and magical, giant sharks. Even though these spirits were dreaded, a person who survived an encounter with such an evil force would be blessed with good luck and wealth for the rest of his life. People often went out of the way to find evil spirits in order to prove their own bravery.

The animals that people hunted and fished for food possessed spirits that would inflict harm if not treated with the proper respect. Salmon bones had to be carefully returned to the place where the fish was caught so the Salmon People inhabiting the river bottoms would not be offended and would continue to offer themselves in fish form to human beings who needed them for food. Sometimes showing respect for an animal required wear-

OPPOSITE: HAIDA SHAMANS IN CEREMONIAL DRESS. **ABOVE**: TLINGIT MEN OFTEN CARVED THE FIGURE OF LAND-OTTER-MAN—THE ANIMAL SPIRIT BELIEVED TO RESCUE THE SOULS OF DROWNING PEOPLE AND TURN THEM INTO LAND OTTERS—INTO THE PROWS OF THEIR WAR CANOES TO ENSURE THEIR CREW'S SAFETY.

ing a certain design of face paint or saying certain prayers before a hunt. Often a specific hunting season was initiated with a ceremony like the First Salmon Rite, in which everyone fasted, prayed, and gave thanks in advance for the bountiful harvest they hoped to receive.

Of all the animals, wolves had the strongest positive supernatural powers, both because they were excellent hunters and because many cultures believed they were the reincarnated souls of their dead ancestors. Owls and land otters, on the other hand, were greatly feared because their spirits associated with dead people.

Spirits in Everyday Life

Strong positive spirits could be a tremendous help to people in hunting, waging war, gambling, and even love, but the power of a spirit had to be searched for and earned. This was usually accomplished by coming into contact with one through a trance or dream. Young men sought their guardian spirits in their early teens, ventur-

THANKING THE BEARS

When a man killed a bear and brought it home, his family treated it as a guest of honor. They would greet the bear with a formal welcoming speech, give it a hat, and shower it with sacred eagle down. Treating the animal with all the respect they would show an honored guest, the family would even place it in a seat of honor and offer it food for one or two days. These actions were taken so that the bear's spirit would not be offended and so that it would return to the area in bear form.

Spirits gave certain members of each family special knowledge. The hunter possessed secret hunting rituals, the canoe maker had tricks to keep his hulls from cracking, and woodworkers learned how to split planks perfectly from a cedar log. Sometimes certain knowledge or power were given to only one clan, which thereafter claimed undisputed sole ownership of it.

Shamans and Sorcerers

A small number of men, known as "shamans," were much more sensitive to the spirit powers than others. Villagers would seek out shamans to predict the future and to influence aspects of their lives such as love, war, health, hunting, and gambling. Since very few people possessed shamanistic powers, shamans were considered an elite group apart from the rest of the village. They lived in houses separate from other villagers, and when they died they were buried in remote areas by themselves.

Shamans received their special powers during the vision quest. Children in families that had a tradition of shamanism were encouraged to prepare for this event more intensely than others, but family affiliation was no guarantee that one was capable of becoming a shaman.

After a young shaman had completed his vision quest, he underwent a rigorous training period that usually lasted several years. In some cultures, he was allowed to see only other shamans during this period. A Kwakiutl shaman-in-training had to

ing out into the wilderness on their vision quests. The fasting, prayer, and ice baths that preceded the vision quest were spiritual rituals that would continue throughout a person's life.

It was believed that spirits were offended by human odors, so baths were a primary way of paying respect. Bathing for this purpose entailed sitting in ice cold water for several hours, three or four days in a row. Following each bath, the person would rub himself vigorously with branches or plant stems to restore his circulation and to disguise the human scent of his body. The severity of these baths, coupled with long periods of fasting, helped bring on the semiconscious trance state in which people could have contact with the spirits.

ABOVE: A HAIDA SHAMAN'S RATTLE CARVED IN THE FORM OF A HEAD WITH A HUMAN FIGURE LYING ACROSS THE TOP

dance in four successive winter ceremonials before he was considered ready to practice as a shaman. He learned to carve the traditional shaman masks, rattles, and amulets; to concoct healing herbal potions; and to diagnose and treat various illnesses. At the conclusion of the young man's training, his relatives gave a feast in his honor announcing his status as a full shaman.

Shamans had curative powers, but they were usually called upon only after family herbal remedies or magic had failed. People believed that illnesses stemmed from one of two sources: evil spirits or sorcery. The shaman's first job was to diagnose which of these two forces was responsible. If the illness was caused by sorcery, there would be a foreign object, such as two bone splinters tied together with human hair, on or in the patient's body, sent by someone who wished the patient harm. Otherwise, an evil spirit was to blame. The shaman would determine the cause of the illness by going into a trance and "seeing" through the patient's body.

There were hundreds of different cures, but almost all began with asking for the assistance of positive super-

A TLINGIT SHAMAN GOES INTO A TRANCE TO DIAG-
NOSE AN ILL PATIENT.

natural powers. After diagnosing the illness, the shaman would change into special clothing and paint his face with special symbols. Before he started humming and chanting his prayers for spiritual help, he arranged his "tools" within reach of the patient's bed. These usually consisted of a jointed puppet, a skull, a small carved box containing shark teeth and oddly shaped pebbles, a rattle, and other appropriate charms and amulets. A helper beat a monotonous rhythm on a box drum and shook a rattle until the shaman went into his trance.

If the illness was caused by evil spirits, the shaman might instruct the patient on how to "dance" it away. If the patient was too ill, the shaman might go into a trance, enter the patient's body, and then drive the spirit away while the drum continued its hypnotic beat.

If the source of illness was an evil object wished into the patient by a sorcerer, the shaman would appear to reach inside the patient and fight with the object's magical powers to pull it out. Then he would hold up a ball of eagle down soaked in blood to show that he had removed the object. Some people knew the ball of down was not really the poisoning object, but they understood that it was a symbol of the evil magic that had been removed from the patient's body.

Although curing patients was an important and dramatic function of a shaman, it was by no means his only service. He was also consulted in cases of soul loss. Northwest Coast peoples believed that a person's soul left his body at night to travel out into the Other World where dreams originated. Sometimes it traveled so far that it could not return before dawn. The soul also could be stolen by evil spirits or sorcerers. Losing one's soul did not mean instant death, just a slow draining of life energy. If the sufferer waited too long before seeking a cure, his soul might go to the Land-of-the-Forever-Dead, and not even a shaman could get it back. Even worse, the person would never be able to be reincarnated.

Some shamans had the ability to travel to the Other World, although it was a long and dangerous journey. Often the shaman asked strong men to wrap a rope around his chest and stay with him while he went into his trance in case something went wrong and he needed to be pulled back from the land of the dead. If he found the lost soul, he carried it back with him in a "soul-catcher," an ivory or bone amulet with holes on each end. Then he would return the soul to its owner.

❦ TOP: THE HATS OF TLINGIT SHAMANS WERE OFTEN MADE OF WOVEN SPLIT SPRUCE ROOTS, THEN EMBROIDERED WITH STRAW AND DECORATED WITH ANIMAL DESIGNS. **ABOVE:** BONE AND SHELL SOUL-CATCHERS WERE THE MOST IMPORTANT TOOLS USED BY TLINGIT SHAMANS. AFTER FINDING AND CATCHING THE ERRANT SOUL OF AN ILL PATIENT, A SHAMAN SEALED THE SOUL INTO THE SOUL-CATCHER FOR SAFEKEEPING WHILE HE CARRIED IT BACK TO HIS PATIENT.

❦ Dancing Societies and Winter Ceremonies

Because Northwest Coast cultures had no system of writing, myths and legends were passed from one generation to the next by the village storyteller and through plays in which people dressed up as supernatural spirits and danced out the stories in front of an audience of other villagers. These winter ceremonies were put on by secret dancing societies that spent months rehearsing and making costumes. Because members had to pay to get in, only the wealthiest people in the tribe belonged to these secret societies. If a village had more than one dancing society, the groups competed to see who staged the most spectacular and mystical ceremony.

Ceremonial dances were magnificent reenactments, complete with elaborate costumes and frightening masks. While the dramatizations themselves differed from village to village, most winter ceremonies typically started with the sound of whistles announcing the arrival of the spirits. The whistles would also be heard any time a new spirit arrived in the scene. Another common element was that the chief dancer would make a dramatic entrance, such as dropping from a rafter into the middle of the performance area. Often he worked himself up into such a frenzy dancing out the plot to the story that he went into a trance and became, in effect, possessed by a spirit who took over his body.

🜨 PARTICIPANTS IN A BELLA COOLA CEREMONIAL DANCE TRADITIONALLY WORE ANIMAL SPIRIT COSTUMES TO ACT OUT SACRED TRIBAL LEGENDS.

🜨 Myths and Legends

Almost all Northwest Coast cultures had creation myths and animal legends based on the Animal People, also called the Original or First People, who occupied the world when time began. The Animal People were beings who looked like animals but acted like humans. Only the deer were animals as we know them today. The Animal People hunted, fished, lived in lodges, and even had chiefs and slaves. They had names like Porpoise Woman, Otter, Whale, Star, and Wren. Gigantic in size, they possessed supernatural powers that enabled them to change back and forth from animal to human form. Unfortunately, many of the animal people were also selfish and cruel; some were actually monsters.

After a while, the Old One, who had created the Animal People, rolled some mud into beings shaped like humans and then blew on them to make them come alive. These first human beings knew very little about how to survive, and their helplessness made them easy prey for the Animal People. The situation got so bad that the Old One finally sent Coyote, also known as the Trickster, to kill the monsters and evil Animal People and to start teaching the humans the best ways to survive.

The Trickster killed off some monsters and turned others into something useful, such as trees or rock formations. But after some time passed, enough monsters remained to make him take more drastic measures. Transforming them into the animals we know today, he took away the evil Animal People's abilities to speak and live like humans, shrank them down to their present sizes, and deprived them of most of their supernatural abilities. The only power the animals still had was the ability to reincarnate themselves as food for humans.

Coyote changed the good Animal People into human form and they came to be called the Ancients, the ancestors of all of today's Native American tribes.

The Trickster himself is a rather interesting character. In some Northwest Coast cultures he is called Mink, Raven, Bluejay, or Fox instead of Coyote, but whatever his name, there are hundreds of stories of how he went about changing the world. Just like humans today, he had many negative characteristics, including greed, envy, and gluttony, as well as many positive ones, such as charity, loyalty, love, and faith. He could be very serious one minute and totally silly the next, but whatever he did, he was powerful enough to change the world's landscape profoundly. Wherever he camped, springs of water popped up. He could pile up mountains just by moving in his sleep. To give the earth light, he stole the sun from the miser guarding it and threw it up into the sky.

But Northwest Coast mythology is made up of much more than Trickster and transformation stories. Many are parables—the adventures of humans and Animal People

NOOTKAN WOLF DANCE

The Nootkan winter ceremony was based on the Wolf Dance, a beautiful and terrifying play performed in dance form in which the actors (older Wolf society members) wore elaborate costumes and masks to act out a famous animal legend. In the story, a man meets the Wolf People, who demonstrate their powers of reviving the dead by singing magical songs. The person they bring back to life in their demonstration is human, but he is able to assume Wolf form by putting on a Wolf coat. Because of this myth, Nootka people believed that dead men were reincarnated as wolves.

Above: In the Klukawala ceremonials held by a Nootka wolf society, participants wore elaborately painted headdresses in the shapes of stylized wolf heads.

COYOTE TAKES WATER FROM THE FROG PEOPLE

One day, Coyote found a dead deer that had ribs that looked like giant dentalia shells. He picked up one of the ribs and went to see the Frog People, who had dammed up the land's entire supply of water, preventing everyone else from having access to it.

When Coyote reached the Frog People, he dangled the rib before them, saying, "I have a big dentalia shell and I want a very big drink of water." The Frog People said that if he gave them the shell, he could have as much as he wanted. So Coyote handed over the "shell" and stuck his head under the water.

But he drank for a very long time. Wondering what he was up to, the Frog People tried to get him to stop. They did not know that he was not drinking at all but was digging out under their dam.

When Coyote was finished, he thanked the Frog People. Just then, the dam collapsed and all the water rushed down into the valley, forming the creeks, rivers, and waterfalls that still exist today. The Frog People were very angry. "You have taken all the water, Coyote!" they cried. But Coyote replied, "It was not right for you to hoard all of it. Now it is where everyone can have it."

Adapted from American Indian Myths and Legends, *eds. Richard Erdoes and Alfonso Ortiz (New York: Pantheon Books, 1984).*

⚘ THIS MASK HEADDRESS WITH ABALONE INLAYS WAS WORN BY THE CHIEF OF A TSIMSHIAN FROG CLAN.

that teach lessons such as "Do not be boastful; otherwise you may end up just as Deer did" or "Don't hang around with someone you know is no good or he'll get you in trouble just like Mink got his little brother in trouble."

By describing how certain characters built shelters when they were caught in a storm or how they found the best place to hunt seals, some tales helped children learn work and survival skills. Some stories retold the adventures of deceased tribal heroes. Others were told purely as entertainment while men were carving and women were working on basketry or weaving.

🔥 CONCLUSION 🔥
Modern Times

When Europeans first showed up on the Northwest Coast in the late 1600s, they believed they were bringing civilization to a race of barbarians. In reality, they brought disease and exploitation, destroying a culture that was just as spiritually, socially, and artistically rich as their own.

In 1670, the English organized the Hudson's Bay Trading Company to trade with Canadian natives for beaver, seal, and other pelts that European consumers were demanding. In their efforts to monopolize the fur trade, English traders moved west through Canada and ultimately reached the Northwest Coast. Before long, Russian traders sailing down the Alaskan coast from Siberia staked their own claims for the Northwest Coast fur trade. While all these foreigners did their best to exploit local peoples for the furs, the Russians were by far the most ruthless. In 1799, Russia awarded the Russian American Fur company an official monopoly in the Pacific Northwest, but by then the Russians had already reduced the native populations in some areas to one tenth of their original numbers.

The interaction with European fur traders was deadly for two reasons. First of all, they brought with them devastating diseases against which Northwest Coast peoples had no immunity. Smallpox, tuberculosis, measles, bubonic plague, scarlet fever, and typhoid are just a few of the diseases that never existed in North and South America until Europeans brought them. Each epidemic wiped out hundreds, even thousands, of people at a time. But the second change the Europeans brought was even more devastating. They changed Northwest Coast societies from hunting economies to fur-trapping economies. At first, the fur trade seemed to be beneficial to Northwest Coast peoples. Guns made hunting much easier; metal kettles and steel tools were more efficient than stone and bone; cloth, needles, and scissors made sewing much faster; and European tools and paint even enhanced Northwest Coast art.

But soon the herds of caribou and the sea mammals Northwest Coast peoples had always hunted for food were being butchered in such numbers that they virtually disappeared. Native peoples could no longer survive by hunting and fishing for food. Instead, they began to depend on the European trading posts for supplies. The European fur traders kept increasing the prices of supplies to encourage the natives to trap more and more furs. Sometimes the Europeans refused to sell the supplies at all. In other instances, they simply closed their outposts without any warning and moved on. As a result, very many native families starved.

By the nineteenth century, native peoples were in danger of losing their land. In the 1850s, gold was discovered in Washington and Oregon. When miners and settlers poured into the Northwest Coast area, natives fought to keep their lands, but they were doomed to lose. United States troops backed up the settlers' and miners' claims, defeated the natives, and then relocated them to reservations, opening their land to still more settlers.

Reservation life deprived Northwest Coast peoples of their culture and language as well as their lands. Children were forced to speak English and attend militaristic boarding schools. Reservation jobs were scarce, and as a result, most people lived in terrible poverty.

Yet even after the Native Americans lost their lands and were forced onto reservations, Europeans took away the only livelihood that remained for them: fishing. In 1855, the U.S. government promised the relocated peoples that they would be guaranteed off-reservation fishing rights in the Northwest Coast. By the late 1880s, however, fishing poachers took over and eventually blocked natives from using these guaranteed fishing grounds. To make matters worse, by the 1920s sportsmen declared the steelhead trout of Northwest Coast rivers a "game" fish and, in the next few decades, added to the threat against aboriginal fishing rights. The hundreds of dams that the Army Corps of Engineers built in 1948 for utility production as well as logging and industrial developments were also threatening the Northwest Coast environment.

In the 1960s, Native Americans, like many minorities in the United States, became more militant in their fight for civil rights, often taking their battles into the courts. They began to receive opportunities for better education and jobs, moving into cities and assimilating into American culture. Many were rediscovering the richness of their heritages and were writing books and creating art to carry on their cultural traditions. But many more were still living in poverty on reservations.

Northwest coast Indian groups today, like these Seet-Ka-Kwaan ceremonial dancers, take great pride in their heritage and work hard to preserve their unique cultural traditions.

In spite of Supreme Court rulings in the 1960s and 1970s entitling Native Americans to catch half of the harvestable fish in all their guaranteed fishing locations, non-Natives still illegally fish in and pollute the area. In fact, in the 1980s, several organizations were formed to oppose Native American fishing rights officially. On the positive side, there are now numerous sports clubs, religious groups, state governments, and environmental protection organizations that are actively lobbying for aboriginal rights.

❦ World Time Line

8000–7500 B.C. **Northwest Coast:**
Hunting and gathering culture begins as people settle on Queen Charlotte Islands and adjacent strip of Northwest coastline.

The World:
Pleistocene era ends; Ice Age mammals disappear; climate becomes more temperate.

7500–2000 B.C. **Northwest Coast:**
Inhabitants of Northwest Coast use stone tools to become accomplished carvers and canoe builders; develop a hunting, fishing, and gathering culture; build massive gabled houses from logs and planking; establish small permanent settlements on river banks and coastal inlets; and develop social organization based on wealth and class status.

The World:
Neolithic era occurs in Europe (4000–2400 B.C.).

2000–1000 B.C. **Northwest Coast:**
Inhabitants start using bone to make more efficient harpoon points and tools, replacing stone implements; as woodworking methods improve, inhabitants build large oceangoing canoes, and sea-hunting culture develops; as more people settle permanently into certain areas, language groups split into smaller divisions; peoples develop culture rich in art and religious ceremonies.

The World:
King Tutankhamen is buried in Egypt (1323 B.C.); Phoenicians dominate Mediterranean trade.

1000–100 B.C. **Northwest Coast:**
Traders begin traveling up and down Northwest coast and inland along major rivers to trade canoes, blankets, copper, slaves, and other valuable goods.

The World:
Olmec civilization develops in Mexico; King David rules Israelites in the Middle East; Taoism and Buddhism develop in Asia; Greek and Roman cultures flourish; Dead Sea scrolls are written; pottery-making techniques develop in Mexico and American Southwest and spread to other cultures.

A.D. 100–950 **Northwest Coast:**
Individual cultures continue to grow, developing sophisticated weaving and basket-making techniques; trade and art flourish; practice of slavery spreads.

The World:

Christianity and Islam develop in Middle East; Maya civilization flourishes in Mexico; China experiences "Golden Age" under Tang Dynasty; empire of Ghana develops in Africa.

A.D. 950–1500 **Northwest Coast:**

Individual cultures continue to grow; population of Northwest Coast region reaches sixty thousand to seventy thousand inhabitants.

The World:

The Crusades take place in Europe and the Middle East; Genghis Khan leads Mongol invasion of China (1210); Marco Polo explores Asia (1271); the empire of Mali flourishes in Africa; Black Death strikes Europe (1300s); the age of the samurai begins in Japan; Aztecs found capital city of Tenochtitlán (1325); Incas flourish in South America; Timbuktu becomes center of Muslim commerce and culture in Africa; first Europeans arrive in North America.

A.D. 1500–1700 **Northwest Coast:**

Steel woodcarving tools and higher quality paint obtained from Europeans give inhabitants tools to enrich their art.

The World:

Henry VIII rules England (1509–1547); Europeans colonize the Americas; Coronado introduces the horse to the Americas; Mogul Empire flourishes in India; kingdom of Benin reaches its peak in West Africa.

A.D. 1700–1900 **Northwest Coast:**

Captain James Cook returns to Europe with sea otter skins received from Nootka chiefs and sets off European demand for furs; Russians begin exploiting Northwest Coast for furs, changing the hunting-and-fishing economy to a crippling fur-trapping economy; Spanish, English, and U.S. fur traders offer competition to Russians; missionaries and whalers infiltrate Northwest Coast, disrupting lifestyles and economy; thousands of Northwest Coast Natives die from fatal diseases brought by Europeans; art and civilization decline.

The World:

Industrial Revolution is under way in Europe; Europeans continue settlement of American colonies; the United States declares independence (1776); Russia sells Alaskan territory to the United States (1867); Europeans and Asians begin immigrating to the United States.

Glossary

Aleut   A culture inhabiting the string of Aleutian Islands off the southwestern tip of what is today Alaska.

Bella Bella   A mainland Kwakiutl culture.

Bering Land Bridge   A stretch of land that anthropologists believe once connected Siberia with Alaska, over which the first inhabitants of the Americas migrated more than eleven thousand years ago.

Bighouse   A multifamily, gabled house that could hold anywhere from three families to several dozen. (Salish peoples called these dwellings "Longhouses.")

camas   A plant of the lily family with blue flowers whose sweet bulbs were collected and eaten by Northwest Coast peoples.

cedar bark   Bark stripped from young cedar saplings, soaked in salt water, and then beaten until flat so its fibers could be woven on a special loom to create a soft fabric.

Chinook   A group of cultures that lived on Vancouver and Puget Sound Islands and were also scattered along part of the coast of Washington State.

clan   A group of people who claimed to be descendants of the same legendary spirit ancestor and which had its own history, traditions, myths and legends, and crest.

coppers   Shieldlike plaques beaten out of extremely rare, raw copper and engraved with crest designs. Giving a copper to an enemy at a potlatch was a dramatic display of wealth.

cradleboard   A hollowed-out cedar board filled with soft, shredded cedar bark, which mothers used to carry their infants on their backs.

dentalia   Extremely rare, tiny white shells found only in deep water off the coast of Vancouver, used as shell money for trade and for decoration on earrings and necklaces.

Haida   A group of cultures that lived on the Queen Charlotte Islands, off the Northwest Coast, who were feared by other Northwest Coast peoples because of their daring war exploits and slave raids.

Heiltsuk   A mainland Kwakiutal culture.

Hupa   A culture group living in the southern part of the Northwest Coast region in an area south from Puget Sound to northern California.

Inuit — A culture (also known as Eskimo) inhabiting the frigid arctic and subartic regions of northern Canada and Alaska.

Karok — A group living in the southern part of the Northwest Coast region in an area south from Puget Sound to northern California.

Kwakiutl — A mainland group of Northwest Coast cultures that included the Bella Bella and the Heiltsuk tribes.

Longhouse — See "Bighouse"

maiden feast — A solemn occasion to mark a girl's passing into adulthood, for which the girl spent many months in spiritual preparation.

Nootka — A group of about twenty feared and aggressive cultures who lived along the coast from the Alaskan Panhandle south to Puget Sound.

potlatch — A feast given to celebrate any sort of occasion, at which the host distributed extravagant gifts to his guests (friends *and* enemies) to demonstrate his own wealth and high status.

Salish — A group of cultures that lived on Vancouver and Puget Sound islands and were also scattered along part of the coast of Washington State.

shaman — A man with special spiritual powers to diagnose and heal the sick, retrieve lost souls, rid people of black magic, foretell the future, and aid the tribe in times of war.

Tlingit — The northernmost group of Northwest Coast Indians, living along the southern Alaskan coast. They had fourteen subgroups living in about fifty villages.

Tsimshian — Northwest Coast cultures (including the Niska on the Nass River and the Gitskan on the Skeena River) just south of the Tlingit living along the southern Alaskan coast. They inhabited both coastal and inland river villages.

vision quest — A spiritual journey made by teenage boys (and sometimes girls) to experience visions that revealed their guardian spirits and their roles in life.

williwaws — Occasional fierce winter winds that brought sudden subfreezing temperatures to the Northwest Coast region.

Yurok — A group living in the southern part of the Northwest Coast region in an area south from Puget Sound to northern California.

✹ Bibliography

Campbell, Joseph. *Historical Atlas of World Mythology*, vols. 1, 2, and 3. New York: Harper & Row, 1988.

Clark, Elizabeth Ella. *Indian Legends of the Pacific Northwest*. Berkeley, Calif.: University of California Press, 1953.

Collison, Frank, ed. *Yakoun, River of Life*. Massett, British Columbia: Council of the Haida Nation, 1990.

Cultural History in British Columbia. Vancouver, British Columbia: BC Studies, 1993.

Dumond, Don E. *The Eskimos and Aleuts*. London: Thames and Hudson, 1987.

Eastman, Carol M. *Gyaehlingaay: Traditions, Tales, and Images of the Kaigani Haida*. Seattle: Burke Museum Publications, 1991.

Emmons, George Thornton. *The Tlingit Indians*. New York: American Museum of Natural History, 1991.

Erdoes, Richard, and Alfonso Ortiz. *American Indian Myths and Legends*. New York: Pantheon Books, 1984.

Fitzhugh, William W., and Valerie Chaussonnet, eds. *Anthropology of the North Pacific Rim*. Washington, D.C.: Smithsonian Institution Press, 1994.

From the Land of the Totem Poles: The Northwest Coast Indian Art Collection at the American Museum of Natural History. Seattle: University of Washington Press, 1991.

Griffin-Pierce, Trudy. *The Encyclopedia of Native America*. New York: Penguin, 1995.

Hilm, Bill. *The Box of Daylight: Northwest Coast Indian Art*. Seattle: University of Washington Press, 1983.

Osinski, Alice. *The Tlingit*. Chicago: Childrens Press, 1990.

Ruby, Robert H. *A Guide to the Indian Tribes of the Pacific Northwest*. Norman, Okla.: University of Oklahoma Press, 1992.

Stewart, Hilary. *Looking at Totem Poles*. Seattle: University of Washington Press, 1993.

Index

Page numbers in *italics* refer to photographs and illustrations.

Photography Credits

Front jacket photograph: Archive Photos: ©Jeff Greenberg

American Museum of Natural History/Courtesy Deparment Library Services: Neg. #3181: p. 30 bottom; Neg. #3155: p. 32 bottom; Neg. #336105: p. 34; Neg. #337569/O. Bauer & P. Hollenbeck: p. 26; Neg. #4930/ Craig Chesek: p. 29 right,

Neg. #4703: p. 31; Neg. #338303/E. Dossetter: p. 24, Neg. #32960: p. 48; G.T. Emmons/Neg. #337541: p. 33; Neg. #336116/O.C. Hastings:

p. 40; Neg. #1553/A.A. Jansson: p. 14; Neg. #15111/Julius Kirschner: p. 20; Neg. #3843/ S.S. Myers: p. 41; Neg. #1572/ Alex Rota: p. 43; Neg. #46093/ Harland Smith: p. 39 top

Anchorage Museum of History and Art: pp. 18, 22, 25, 51

Archive Photos: p. 53; ©Hirz: p. 28; ©Jeff Greenberg: pp. 42 right, 57

Art Resource: p. 42 left; Werner Forman Archive: pp. 5 both, 8, 10, 12, 13 both, 19, 21, 23, 27, 29 left, 30 top, 36 left, 39 bottom, 44, 45, 47 both, 49, 50, 52 both, 54, 55

FPG International: p. 11; ©Lee Foster: p. 2

Leo de Wys: ©Grant Haller: p. 15

Courtesy of The National Museum of the American Indian/ Smithsonian Institution: Neg. #14898: p. 32 top

Emilya Naymark: All map illustrations

Tony Stone Images: ©Daniel J. Cox: p. 36 right; ©Johnny Johnson: p. 17; ©Art Wolfe: p. 9